ALSO BY JEFF MOSS

with illustrations by Chris Demarest

Bob and Jack: A Boy and His Yak

The Butterfly Jar

The Other Side of the Door

HIERONYMUS WHITE

A Bird Who Believed That
He Always Was Right

by Jeff Moss

Illustrated by Chris Demarest

BALLANTINE BOOKS • NEW YORK

Moss, Jeffrey.
Hieronymus White / Jeff Moss.
p. cm.
ISBN 0-345-38590-X
1. Perfection—Poetry. 2. Family—Poetry. 3. Birds—Poetry. I. Title.
PS3563.O88458H5   1994
811'.54—dc20   94-15566
CIP

Manufactured in the United States of America
First Edition: November 1994
10 9 8 7 6 5 4 3 2 1

In Memory Of
Celia, Joe, Essie, Jack
and
Papa Arnold

HIERONYMUS WHITE

I

This is the story of Hieronymus White,
A bird who believed that he always was right.

From the time he was young, till his feathers turned gray,

He was certain his way was the only true way.

From the food that he ate, to the way that he dressed,

Hieronymus thought that he always knew best.

He ate lots of brown bread to make himself strong.

He wore warm, furry hats on his head all year long.

And of course, to Hieronymus, one thing was true—

All the world should eat brown bread and wear warm hats, too.

So he bought the best hats made of fine woolen thread,

And the best marmalade for his famous brown bread.

But his sureness was not just for things that he bought,

He was equally certain of things that he thought.

He believed that all children should learn how to fly,

As soon as they could, and as far and as high.

He was certain, although he was round-the-world known,

One should wash one's own shirts and eat breakfast alone.

He was always an expert, whatever the task.
He would share his advice, there was no need to ask.
When his children came down with a fever or chills,
He'd order the doctor to choose different pills.
When the postman delivered a package or letter,
Hieronymus told him how he could do better.
He approached every issue so confidently,
He'd seem shocked at the thought that you might not agree.
Yes, all through a life that was famous and long,
Hieronymus thought that he couldn't be wrong,
Till one day, late in life, when his feathers were thinning.

So now let's go back to the very beginning . . .

This is the story of Hieronymus White,
A bird who believed that he always was right.

II

More than a hundred long years ago,
In a land not at all like the land that we know,
A pair of young birds were joined in life—
Armand was the husband and Lili, the wife.
(These two would become, on a far-distant night,
The father and mother of Hieronymus White.)

But now they were young, and they lived in a land
Full of difficult things they could not understand.
In this land there were birds who were loud, rough and strong,
Who said, "If you're not like us, you don't belong.
You must march to our music and sing to our song,
Or else you'll be sorry before very long.
You must eat what we eat and drink what we drink.
You must cough when we cough and blink when we blink,
You must look the way we look and think what we think.
Or else you'll be sorry as quick as a wink."

Once, as Armand and Lili came home from their shop,
A group of these birds blocked their way and cried, "Stop!"
They pushed Armand down and did not let him speak.
They made fun of the shape of the tip of his beak,
Crying, "Look at that bird! What a sight, what a nerve!
For our beaks are straight and his has a curve!"
They poked Lili's feathers and called her a name,
Crying, "Look at our feathers! Yours aren't the same!"
"Green feathers!" they cried. "Your feathers are wrong!
It's perfectly clear that you just don't belong!"
They tweaked them and pinched them and when they were done,
They ran away laughing as if it were fun.

If you disagreed with what they thought was right,
These birds banged on your door in the middle of the night
And scared you so badly your skin felt all chilly.
And that's what they did to Armand and Lili.

So one afternoon in the park, near a tree,
Armand turned to Lili and spoke quietly.
He said, "If we hope to have children one day,
For them to be happy, we must move away."
That day, the young couple decided to fly
To a new land they'd heard of across the big sky.
They hadn't much money but they had young, strong wings.
They bought one small suitcase and packed a few things.
They closed up their shop and they tied up loose ends
And said their good-byes to a very few friends.

Then one cool autumn morning, Lili and Armand
Stretched their wings and flew off toward a new life beyond.

III

When you move to a school in a far-away city
And you're not a great athlete, or handsome or pretty,
If you're just kind of regular, it can be hard
To be the new kid in a strange new school yard.

That's a bit like what happened to Lili and Armand.
Like two little fish in a great big new pond,
They arrived fresh and ready to greet the new land,
And start the new life they had hoped for and planned.

They each got a job, but the hours were long,
And although they were young and determined and strong,
Still, sometimes they struggled with too little pay,
And were sometimes discouraged at the end of a day.

Still, life was better than it had been before,
Without any loud night-time knocks on the door.
And when several years passed, they could buy a small store
Where they worked even harder and saved a bit more,
Till they bought a small house with one extra room
And a little square garden where flowers could bloom.

And then, in late summer, on a warm purple night,
As the evening's first star shed its flickering light,
A baby was born—a tiny boy bird
Who let out a peep loud enough to be heard.

He looked round the room, let out one more peep,
Then he nestled up close and fell fast asleep,
Snuggling deep into Lili's soft feathery side.
Armand stood nearby. They were both filled with pride,
And they both felt a gladness they never had known,
For they now had a home and a child of their own.

The very next morning, the proud dad and mother
Sat with their baby and said to each other,
"Our son will be different, he won't be the same.
Let's be sure that we give him the very best name."

So they sat in the garden and gave it a try,
And considered some names as the morning passed by.

First they thought about George. Then they thought about Bill.
Then Tom, Steve, and Jason, then Tyler, then Phil.
They thought about Brian and Carlos and Stan,
And Sammy and Frederic and Adam and Dan.
But there wasn't one name that they liked in that bunch.
So they stopped for a while for a quick bite of lunch.
Then they thought about Robert and Walter and Harry,
And Norman and Louis and Peter and Larry,
And Herb and Kareem and Timmy and Thor,
And maybe a hundred and thirty-two more.

"Too bad," Lili sighed. "This is really a shame.
If it keeps up, we'll soon have a son with no name,
And with no name at all, he will just be anonymous."
"I've got it!" cried Armand. "Let's call him Hieronymus!"
And that seemed a fine name, and proper and right.
So that's what they called him—Hieronymus White.
That night they talked of their dreams for their son.
"He'll do things far greater than we've ever done,"
Lili said. "He'll be wise, and his heart will be strong. . . .
And *no one* will tell him his feathers are wrong!"
"Or his thoughts!" Armand cried. "He will sing his own song,
And he'll *never* be told that he doesn't belong!"

Lili said, "He'll be better, he'll outshine the rest."
"Not just better," cried Armand. "Our son will be best!"

Armand and Lili had such plans and schemes
For their tiny boy bird, so many big dreams.
Would their dreams all come true? Surely, chances were slight.
But then this is the story of Hieronymus White . . .

IV

Young Hieronymus' looks were not in dispute—
He was not all that handsome or even that cute.

His body was small and he didn't look strong,
You wouldn't glance twice at him hopping along.
He was just a plain bird when he was earthbound.
But something else happened when his feet left the ground.
Perhaps his long wings were built perfectly right
To go with his weight, and his shape, and his height.
Perhaps his tail-feathers were perfectly made
To dive through the wind, and to soar unafraid.
What's sure is: things happen and no one knows why—
And Hieronymus White . . . Oh, how he could fly!

From the earliest days that he took to the air,
Neighbors' beaks would fall open, their eyes would just stare
At the beautiful, graceful, inspiring sight
Of the still-so-young bird named Hieronymous White.
Strangers would gasp as they watched from the ground.
"He's amazing!" they cried. "He's the best bird around!"

Yet not everyone was so free with their praise.
His parents would watch him with purposeful gaze,
And though his mistakes were ever so slight,
They would point out each one to Hieronymus White.
When Hieronymus landed and ran to Armand,
His father might frown and sternly respond,
"Your wing tilted left when it should have gone right.
And your figure-eight loop, was it perfect? Not quite."

When he landed near Lili on a cold rainy day,
His mother reacted in a similar way:
"It's cold way up there. Next time, wear your sweater!
That way you'll fly even higher and better!"

But sometimes his parents spoke more quietly,
Saying, "Son, you must be everything you can be.
Here is the lesson that we want to teach you:
If it's you who flies highest, then no one can reach you
To hurt you or tease you or tell you you're wrong,
To make you feel sad and not let you belong."

So almost no matter what time you passed by,
You could pause for a moment and see in the sky
A bird who'd grow up to be round-the-world known,
Silently circling apart and alone,
With no one to help him or share his delight,
Alone in the sky, young Hieronymus White.

V

Before very long, the time came to start school.
Hieronymus' parents sat him down on a stool.
"Speak right out!" said Armand. "Just forget any shyness!"
"You'll get all A's!" said Lili. "At worst, one A minus."

Hieronymus worked hard and got A's on each test.
In class he would answer ahead of the rest.

He answered so often it wasn't polite,
So often his teacher, at certain times, might
Say, "Can I have an answer, who cares wrong or right,
From anyone else but Hieronymus White?"

He kept flying higher and won his first fame,
And people began to have heard of his name.
In the third grade, a magazine asked for his views,
In the fourth, he appeared on the afternoon news.

In the fifth, as time passed, and his fame slowly grew,
He began to be sure about other things, too.
He announced it was best if you washed your own shirt,
And that chewy brown bread was the finest dessert.
Why he believed these things, nobody knew.
But Hieronymus surely believed they were true.
He announced every preference as if it were fact.
Sureness was not what Hieronymus lacked.

Now, when someone behaves as if he's always right,
And he's proud and he's stubborn, and not that polite,
And the afternoon news wants to film him in flight,
And his teachers all think he's exceptionally bright—
Well, for everyone else, that's a hard nut to bite,
So . . . not everyone liked Hieronymus White.

"Let him fly," they said, "thirty times high as a tree.
We'd rather play baseball or watch our TV.
We think he's as boring as cold noodle soup.
Who cares for his soaring or looping the loop
Or his special excuses that let him miss gym?
Hieronymus White! Who cares about him?"

And so, though Hieronymus sang his own song,
Though his mind and his heart were determined and strong,
Still, every so often, he'd sense something wrong,
And he'd feel, just a bit . . . like he didn't belong.
And that was a feeling that didn't seem right,
So it didn't stay long with Hieronymus White.

VI

Hieronymus did not have a sister or brother.
His family contained just his father and mother.
They worked hard all day and when they were done,
They didn't have much time to spend with their son.
No time to read books or sing songs or take walks,
And no time for father-or-motherly talks.

All their spare time went to study his flight,
And to point out the things that they thought weren't right.
And all their spare money, from the drawer in the dresser,
Went to hire Hieronymus' flying professor.
So when Christmastime came, Hieronymus did not
Get the same kind of presents the other birds got.
Instead, every Christmas, his usual gift
Would be one extra lesson from Professor von Schmift.

Still, there was a Christmas he'd always remember.
His parents worked long hours one cold December.
On Christmas morning, when Hieronymus came down,
They gave him a box that was simple and brown.
He could feel his heart beating as he peeked inside,
At first just a crack, then he opened it wide.
Inside was a hat, warm and fleecy and green.
"Papa, Mama!" he cried. "It's the best hat I've seen!"
It had soft furry flaps that would cover his ears.
It would keep a small bird warm and cozy for years.

Hieronymus wore the hat all winter through.
Through springtime he wore it, and summertime, too.
His schoolmates would tease him and grab at the hat.
He'd clutch it tight, crying, "No, don't you touch that!"
He wore the hat proudly, by day and by night,
Long after the color was no longer bright,
Past the time it was torn in an after-school fight,
Till grown-up and world-known, he wore it in flight
And there could be no more familiar a sight
Than the famous green hat of Hieronymus White.

VII

Hieronymus grew as time hurried by fast.
Soon school days were over and childhood had passed.
He flew for large crowds, with success, to be sure.
He flew on TV, then a twelve-country tour.

With impossible swoops and incredible flips,
With remarkable loops and undo-able dips,
Thousands of wings clapped in each big arena
From Northwest Missouri to South Argentina.
His life became full of appointments and plans,

With no time for friends, but now he had fans.
Hieronymus Fan Clubs were writing him letters,
And wearing Hieronymus shirts, hats, and sweaters.
They wanted his picture to hang on the wall.
He hired a manager to take care of it all.

Then, in addition, he'd sometimes employ
Some accountants to count, and some lawyers to loy,
And barbers to make sure his feathers were trim,
And trainers to exercise with in the gym.
And all of the birds round Hieronymus White
Told him, all of the time, that he always was right.
If he gazed at the sun and said, "What a dark night,"
There were those who'd agree with Hieronymus White.
Soon he claimed to know better than most everyone
About each and everything under the sun.
About music, or shoes, or the history of apes,
About baseball, or cars, or the way to eat grapes.
He wouldn't let anyone make a suggestion,
He knew all the answers, whatever the question.

But the truth is: down-deep, far too down-deep to show it—
In fact, so down-deep he might not even know it,
Hieronymus White, just like every bird,
Needed help and advice and a good thoughtful word.

And then one rare night, at the Garden Arena,
Hieronymus White met a bird named Sabrina.
She was kind and intelligent, patient and wise,
With a soft, knowing look in her honest gray eyes.
Though she knew he believed that he always was right,
From that first night, Sabrina loved Hieronymus White.

And he soon loved her, too, in his own special way.
He would show her his new flying movements each day.
He trusted Sabrina, he took her advice,
Though often she might have to mention things twice.
She'd say: "Don't you think that this way might be better?"
She'd suggest a new swoop, or a new style of sweater.
At first, he would take her idea and pooh-pooh it.
He'd say, "That idea? Oh, I already knew it."
Or, "What an idea! Why, there's nothing to it."
Then later, he'd quietly go off and do it.
Then he'd say to Sabrina, "These ideas are fine.
I like the new style of this sweater's design.
And I'll swoop to the left here, not just a straight line.
I'm really quite proud of these ideas of mine."
Then Sabrina would nod and say, "Hmm, yes, you're right,"
And know she'd been helpful to Hieronymus White.

He sent her a daisy from his own flower bed,
And several months later, the two of them wed.
Then the following June, two new lives were begun.
Sabrina gave birth to a daughter and son.
The girl was Amanda, the boy was named Dwight,
The twins of Sabrina and Hieronymus White.

VIII

World-famous, Hieronymus was now at his peak.
Day after day and week after week,
Crowds begged him to fly and implored him to speak,
And cheered at the sight of the tip of his beak.
(These were the years when he dove through the hoop,
In his Super Quadruple Loop-o'-the-loop.)

He didn't have much time for being a father.
He found changing diapers a bit of a bother.
He didn't quite understand how to have fun
With a small drooly daughter and a small gurgly son.

Still, when he was home with Amanda and Dwight,
Hieronymus knew that he always was right.
He told both his children what books they should read,
What clothes they should wear, and what food they would need.

Sometimes, Sunday mornings at seven o'clock,
He'd call them outside to the big backyard rock.
"If there's one thing I know, it's that all birds should fly
As soon as they can and as far and as high,"
Hieronymus said to Amanda and Dwight.
"So try to fly higher, and better, and right."
But though each of his children was quite a good flier,
Hieronymus wanted still better and higher.
"That takeoff's too slow! That loop is too wide!"
Are some of the things Hieronymus cried.

The twins tried to please him, they tried and they tried.
But Hieronymus never was quite satisfied.
He'd return to his work and continue his quest
Of trying to be even better than best.

He'd bought Armand and Lili a big house nearby.
They'd visit for dinner or come watch him fly.
And though their son now was a world-famous name,
They'd still treat Hieronymus exactly the same.
"That Super Quadruple Loop-o'-the-loop,
Why not add a somersault in the last swoop?
It will be more exciting when you dive through the hoop,"
Armand would say sharply, while sipping his soup.

And so years kept passing, the way that years do.
The grown-ups got older, the children all grew,
Till Armand couldn't hear well and walked with a cane,
And Lili caught a sickness that's hard to explain.
And one day, at a very old age, Lili died.
The next year Armand was laid close by her side.
Dwight and Amanda became fully grown,
They each had a home and a job of their own.
The days were more quiet and serious now.
Even Hieronymus seemed older somehow.
Some of his head-feathers soon would grow thin.
The last part of life was about to begin,
With good things and hard things lying just out of sight
For the world-famous bird named Hieronymus White.

IX

Soon feathers turned gray on Hieronymus' face,
And his days seemed to move at a not-so-fast pace.
He travelled less often, less time on the run,
And the fun that he had now was more quiet fun.

He spent less time flying and more on the ground.
Some hours for relaxing and reading were found.
He bought a new telescope to gaze at the stars.
A publisher asked him to write his memoirs.
Then Dwight and Amanda each met someone,
And he went to the weddings of his daughter and son.
And soon after that, most surprising to find,
The thought of a grandchild was high on his mind.
He knew he'd missed time with Amanda and Dwight
When they were small children. Perhaps now there might
Be a child he could love, to be cared for and taught.
And that was Hieronymus' dream, wish, and thought.

So with far more excitement than he could remember,
He learned that a baby was due in December.
He counted the days till the special news came
On December 19th. Selene was her name.
He and Sabrina set off for Amanda's,
With bright-blooming flowers and two huge stuffed pandas.
From the trip's start to finish, he couldn't refrain
From chatting to birds that he met on the train:
"I have a new grandchild to care for and love!
We'll do all the fine things I've been dreaming of.
We'll read books together, play games and sing songs.
I'll help her to feel like she always belongs.
I'll teach her to fly. Oh, how great she will be!
I'll teach her to fly even higher than me!"

He arrived at Amanda's house. On the veranda,
He put down the flowers and dropped each stuffed panda
On an old rocking chair. Then he hurried inside,
And rushed to the bedroom, his wings open wide.

"It's me, it's your Grandpa!" Hieronymus cried.

He saw his granddaughter, and his heart filled with pride.

The newborn bird lay with Amanda in bed.

"Come fly to Grandpa!" Hieronymus said.

"Come fly to Grandpa! What's taking so long?

You've got to start early if you want to be strong.

You must set your own rhythm and sing your own song!"

Then he looked at Amanda, and something was wrong.

With her beak slightly open, her gray eyes so sad,
Amanda's face spoke of news that was bad.
Hieronymus slowly bent over Selene,
And then he saw something that he hadn't seen.
One wing seemed to fold where it should have been straight,
Like a gateway that stands with a half-missing gate.
It was less than a wing, almost no wing at all.
Otherwise, she was perfect and peaceful and small.
But, in that instant, Hieronymus knew
That something too hard to imagine was true.
He knew that things happen and no one knows why,
And he knew that the newborn bird never would fly.

His heart hurt more deeply than he'd ever known.
He looked down at the baby and the child of his own.
Then he reached toward Amanda and touched her soft face,
He brushed one stray cheek-feather back into place.
He held still for a moment. Then he turned toward Selene,
And watched as she slept in a newborn bird's dream.
He stood without moving at the side of the bed.
Then he reached toward Selene and lowered his head,
And he kissed her so softly, so sweet, and so light.
He kissed her more gently than anyone might,
Not a kiss you'd expect from Hieronymus White.
Then he went from the room, out into the night.

He sat on the porch in the old rocking chair.
With his eyes closed, he breathed in the sharp winter air.
He sat as the sun set and as the moon rose.
He sat as the stars filled the sky in repose.

And sitting alone through the long winter night,
Under thousands of pinpoints of far-flickering light,
He knew that no one could always be right,
And something changed inside Hieronymus White.

X

In the following years, no one would have foreseen
The joy that Hieronymus gained from Selene.
As for Selene, nothing brought her delight
Like the hours she spent with Hieronymus White.
On her Grandpapa's lap in the old rocking chair,
There'd be nothing so cozy as snuggling there.
They might read a book, or a song would be sung,
Or he'd tell her a story of when he was young.

They'd have conversations and eat their brown bread.
He'd ask her opinion and hear what she said.
Whatever the subject, Hieronymus White
Wanted to know what Selene thought was right.
On some days, new stories were told by Selene
About places she'd visit or people she'd seen.
He asked her to write down the stories she'd tell.
This was something Selene did especially well.
Then after the stories, they'd talk or they'd rest
Till at last came the moment Selene loved the best.
He'd put on his hat, old and tattered and green,
And Hieronymus White would fly just for Selene.
He'd seem to leap straight forward into the sky.
Then he'd swoop and he'd circle, and come gliding by.
He'd soar steep above her and sail smooth and high.

And then it would happen. Without knowing why,
It somehow would seem that Selene, too, could fly.
She knew she was with him, together in flight,
As her heart sailed the sky with Hieronymus White.

XI

It was many years later, Selene now was grown.
She'd become a young writer, with books of her own.
Her grandpa was gone now, he'd finished his flight.
But Selene still thought of Hieronymus White.

As she was straightening the attic one day,
Under a pile of things nestled away,
The corner of something brown captured her eye.
She moved an old lamp and a suitcase nearby,
And pulled out a simple brown box tied with string.
Selene felt her heart beating under her wing
As she saw the faint writing, in script large and clean:
"For my granddaughter, always, with love, to Selene."
She untied the box and looked slowly inside,
At first just a crack, then she opened it wide . . .
It was torn, it was faded, a pale shade of green.

You'd never have thought that it once could have been
As fine a new hat as a young bird had seen.

Her heart filled with memories of when she was small,
When her Grandpapa's flying was the best thing of all.

Then she stood still and quiet and imagined a day
In the near-distant future, not that far away,
When a son of her own might circle in flight,
Wearing the hat as he soared to full height
On a crisp winter morning, sparkling and bright.
And then, as she tucked him in bed late that night,
She would add one more blanket and turn off the light,
And tell him the story of Hieronymus White.

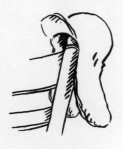

Thanks and more thanks to Linda Grey, Esther Newberg and Annie Boylan, for their help in the making of this book; and to Matthew Shear, for putting it together with care, patience, and good humor.

J.M.

JEFF MOSS was one of the original creators of *Sesame Street*. He has served as head writer and composer-lyricist on the show, and he has won thirteen Emmys and written the songs for four Grammy-winning records. Moss's music and lyrics for *The Muppets Take Manhattan* earned him an Academy Award nomination. He is the author of two collections of poetry, *The Butterfly Jar* and *The Other Side of the Door*, and the beloved children's book *Bob and Jack: A Boy and His Yak*. Moss helped create some of television's most memorable characters, including Cookie Monster and Oscar the Grouch. His hit songs include "Rubber Duckie," "I Love Trash," "The People in Your Neighborhood," and "I Don't Want to Live on the Moon."

CHRIS DEMAREST is the author and illustrator of several books, including *My Little Red Car*, a 1992 Parents' Choice Award winner, and *Lindbergh*, a 1993 School Library Journal Best Book. He is the illustrator of Jeff Moss's *Bob and Jack: A Boy and His Yak*, *The Butterfly Jar*, and *The Other Side of the Door*.